JESSICA JONES:

Brian Michael Bendis
WRITER

Michael Gaydos
ARTIST

Matt Hollingsworth
COLORIST

Mark Bagley, Al Vey & Dean White
DREAM SEQUENCE

Richard Starkings & Comicraft's Wes Abbott & Jason Levine (#10 & #16) and Cory Petit (#17 & #21)
LETTERERS

David Mack
COVER ART

Stuart Moore, Joe Quesada & C.B. Cebulski
EDITORS

Kelly Lamy
ASSOCIATE MANAGING EDITOR

Nanci Dakesian
MANAGING EDITOR

ALIaS CREATED BY BRIAN MICHAEL BENDIS & MICHAEL GAYDOS

Collection Editor: Jennifer Grünwald
Assistant Editor: Sarah Brunstad
Associate Managing Editor: Alex Starbuck
Editor, Special Projects: Mark D. Beazley
Senior Editor, Special Projects: Jeff Youngquist
SVP Print, Sales & Marketing: David Gabriel
Book Designer: Jay Bowen

Editor in Chief: Axel Alonso
Chief Creative Officer: Joe Quesada
Publisher: Dan Buckley
Executive Producer: Alan Fine

JESSICA JONES: ALIAS VOL. 3. Contains material originally published in magazine form as ALIAS #10 and #16-21. Second printing 2016. ISBN# 978-0-7851-9857-4. Published by MARVEL WORLDWIDE, INC., a subsidiary of MARVEL ENTERTAINMENT, LLC. OFFICE OF PUBLICATION: 135 West 50th Street, New York, NY 10020. Copyright © 2015 MARVEL No similarity between any of the names, characters, persons, and/ or institutions in this magazine with those of any living or dead person or institution is intended, and any such similarity which may exist is purely coincidental. Printed in the U.S.A. ALAN FINE, President, Marvel Entertainment; DAN BUCKLEY, President, TV, Publishing and Brand Management; JOE QUESADA, Chief Creative Officer; TOM BREVOORT, SVP of Publishing; DAVID BOGART, SVP of Operations & Procurement, Publishing; C.B. CEBULSKI, VP of International Development & Brand Management; DAVID GABRIEL, SVP Print, Sales & Marketing; JIM O'KEEFE, VP of Operations & Logistics; DAN CARR, Executive Director of Publishing Technology; SUSAN CRESPI, Editorial Operations Manager; ALEX MORALES, Publishing Operations Manager; STAN LEE, Chairman Emeritus. For information regarding advertising in Marvel Comics or on Marvel.com, please contact Jonathan Rheingold, VP of Custom Solutions & Ad Sales, at jrheingold@marvel.com. For Marvel subscription inquiries, please call 800-217-9158. Manufactured between 1/6/2016 and 1/25/2016 by R.R. DONNELLEY, INC., SALEM, VA, USA.
10 9 8 7 6 5 4 3 2

PREVIOUSLY IN ALIAS ...

Jessica Jones, a former costumed super hero, is now the owner and sole employee of Alias Investigations, a small private-investigative firm.

After a string of bad relationships, Jessica is fixed up with Scott Lang, a.k.a. Ant-Man. They are early in a potential relationship.

ISSUE #10

RECEPTIONIST
Ms. Jones, can I get you anything?

JESSICA JONES
When is this article from?

RECEPTIONIST
Um -- I'm not sure. There might be a date on it.

JESSICA JONES
Jameson wrote this himself?

RECEPTIONIST
Yes, ma'am, I guess he did.

JESSICA JONES
Didn't realize he'd been in newspapers for so long.

RECEPTIONIST
He's what he likes to call a "lifer." Can I get you anything to drink? Water? Coffee?

JESSICA JONES
No. No, I'm fine.

RECEPTIONIST
Mr. Jameson will be in shortly. He's on a call.

JESSICA JONES
Do you know why he asked me here?

RECEPTIONIST
No. Sorry, I don't. I'm not his personal assistant. I'm just the --

JESSICA JONES
Okay.

RECEPTIONIST
Sorry.

JESSICA JONES
No, it's okay.

□ DAILY 🎺 BUGLE □
NEW YORK'S FINEST DAILY NEWSPAPER

SPIDER-MAN MENACE?

□ DAILY 🎺 BUGLE □
NEW YORK'S FINEST DAILY NEWSPAPER

CAPTAIN AMERICA FOUND!

□ DAILY 🎺 BUGLE □
NEW YORK'S FINEST DAILY NEWSPAPER

KREE-SKRULL WAR ENDS!

J. JONAH JAMESON
Ms. Jones?

JESSICA JONES
Yes.

J. JONAH JAMESON
Jessica Jones?

JESSICA JONES
Yes.

J. JONAH JAMESON
My name is J. Jonah Jameson. I'm the publisher here at the Daily Bugle.

JESSICA JONES
Yes, yes, I know who you are,

J. JONAH JAMESON
Ms. Brant! (One second, Ms. Jones.) Ms. Brant!!

BETTY BRANT
Yes, sir.

J. JONAH JAMESON
What the hell is this?

BETTY BRANT
That's the Metro column.

J. JONAH JAMESON
The hell it is. Tell Hendrickson I want this con artist gone from my news-paper. These <u>damn</u> guys and their <u>damn</u> conservative agendas creeping into every <u>damn</u> corner of my paper. Like I don't know what he's up to.

BETTY BRANT
Yes, sir.

J. JONAH JAMESON
Get Robbie in here.

BETTY BRANT
He's in the archive.

J. JONAH JAMESON
I didn't ask for a Robbie update -- just get him in here.

BETTY BRANT
Yes, sir.

J. JONAH JAMESON
And get Be -- Ms. Brant!!

BETTY BRANT
Yes, sir.

J. JONAH JAMESON
Where'd you go? I was talking.

BETTY BRANT
I went to get Robbie.

J. JONAH JAMESON
I wasn't done. Get Ben Urich in here too.

BETTY BRANT
He's on his smoke break.

J. JONAH JAMESON
Dammit --

BETTY BRANT
Sorry.

J. JONAH JAMESON
Just get him in here.

BETTY BRANT
Yes, sir.

J. JONAH JAMESON
Do you have any employees, Ms. Jones?

JESSICA JONES
No sir.

J. JONAH JAMESON
Count yourself a lucky woman.

J. JONAH JAMESON
I've worked with some investigators -- hired some. Haven't found a one I would let babysit my grandson.

JESSICA JONES
I don't exactly know what I'm supposed to say to that, but --

J. JONAH JAMESON
Robbie -- this is that Jessica Jones person I was talking to you about.

ROBBIE ROBERTSON
Oh. Hi.

JESSICA JONES
Hello.

ROBBIE ROBERTSON
Uh, Jonah, I thought we were going to discuss this further before we made any --

J. JONAH JAMESON
We discussed it enough. We talked it to death.

ROBBIE ROBERTSON
I really --

J. JONAH JAMESON
To death! Robbie's the Editor in Chief. And Jessica Jones here used to dress up like a super hero.

ROBBIE ROBERTSON
Oh.

JESSICA JONES
Well...

ROBBIE ROBERTSON
You did...

JESSICA JONES
I did, but...

ROBBIE ROBERTSON
Who were you?

J. JONAH JAMESON
She was a little number called "Jewel" for a while. Not much to write home about -- no offense, Ms. Jones.

JESSICA JONES
None taken, but...

J. JONAH JAMESON
And then she tried the game as a woman called... "Knightress"?

JESSICA JONES
Yeah. Uh -- not a lot of people know that.

J. JONAH JAMESON
Though I despise your chosen profession, I do admire your going public with your questionable past. I imagine that was somewhat of a hard choice.

JESSICA JONES
Uh, not really. Firstly, I wouldn't use the word "questionable." And truth be told, no one cared either way. But I guess it makes meetings like this a little more interesting.

J. JONAH JAMESON
You guess?

JESSICA JONES
Well, I still don't know what this meeting is about, so...

J. JONAH JAMESON
It's about secret identities. I thought Robbie would find your background a little interesting considering what I am about to offer you.

THE KNIGHTRESS

JESSICA JONES
Uh, what is that you have there?
Is that all about me?

J. JONAH JAMESON
Yes, it's your archive here

JESSICA JONES
My clippings?

J. JONAH JAMESON
Your clippings.

JESSICA JONES
Oh. I hadn't realized I made
the paper so many times.

J. JONAH JAMESON
Ms. Brant!

BETTY BRANT
Yes, sir.

J. JONAH JAMESON
Take this to Xerox and make a copy of it for Ms. Jones. Every paper.

BETTY BRANT
Yes, sir.

JESSICA JONES
Oh, uh, thanks.

J. JONAH JAMESON
Make yourself a little scrapbook. So, Ms. Jones, are the numbers on your web site correct?

JESSICA JONES
You mean my fees?

J. JONAH JAMESON
Yes.

JESSICA JONES
You want to hire me?

J. JONAH JAMESON.
Yes. I -- Ms. Brant!!

ROBBIE ROBERTSON
You just sent her to make copies.

J. JONAH JAMESON
Dammit! Where ś Urich?

ROBBIE ROBERTSON
He's coming. Jonah, can we discuss this a little before --?

J. JONAH JAMESON
What we'd like to do, Ms. Jones, is hire you -- pay you your full wage and have one of my reporters follow you.

JESSICA JONES
Follow me where?

J. JONAH JAMESON
Ben, where were you?

BEN URICH
I didn't know you were --

J. JONAH JAMESON
Sit down. Say hi to Jessica Jones.

BEN URICH
Why is that name familiar?

J. JONAH JAMESON
You can do the niceys later. Jessica is a private investigator. The Daily Bugle is hiring her to find out who Spider-Man really is.

JESSICA JONES
Uh -- what?

J. JONAH JAMESON
Jessica here is going to crack his world in half and you are going to follow her while she does it.

JESSICA JONES
Well, I . . .

J. JONAH JAMESON
What we're hoping for is a series of articles. A real conversation piece to spread over days -- but hey! If all it is is a big red headline -- then all it is is a big red headline.

JESSICA JONES
Um...

J. JONAH JAMESON
The idea came to me over this crap with that Daredevil.

BEN URICH
Jonah, we went over this. He --

J. JONAH JAMESON
That Murdock guy pretending he's a blind shyster. The Globe had that story and they screwed it up. Well, I want to show the world how to crack one of these guys in half.

JESSICA JONES
But, um, Matt Murdock isn't Daredevil. That story is --

BEN URICH
He knows. He's in denial.

J. JONAH JAMESON
I know what you say, Urich -- but I don't see any proof on my desk that backs you up. I don't care who that liar sues or what TV show he goes crying to -- I know in my gut it's a fact. Murdock is Daredevil.

JESSICA JONES
No, it's not.

J. JONAH JAMESON
Oh, and how do you know?

JESSICA JONES
Matt Murdock is my lawyer and I do work for him.

J. JONAH JAMESON
Well, ain't that cozy...

JESSICA JONES
He's blind. What are you --?

J. JONAH JAMESON
It's bull. It's a secret identity. It's a cover.

JESSICA JONES
No, really, he's blind.

J. JONAH JAMESON
Well, you and Urich can start a little super hero love club.

JESSICA JONES
I don't think I get what the anger is about.

J. JONAH JAMESON
It's just frustrating that I am surrounded by this pro-costume --

JESSICA JONES
Pro-costume?

J. JONAH JAMESON
I thought that you of all people -- someone who crashed and burned so miserably at it -- would understand the need to rip that world apart from the inside -- to expose those capes for the two-faced, morally corrupt vigilantes that they are!!

JESSICA JONES
Uh huh...

J. JONAH JAMESON
And this Spider-Man -- I could give two Canadian nickels about Daredevil -- it's this Spider-Man that should've gotten the public spanking. It's Spider-Man that has this coming to him.

JESSICA JONES
Why?

J. JONAH JAMESON
What?

JESSICA JONES
Why does Spider-Man have this coming to him?

J. JONAH JAMESON
That's what you're going to tell me.

JESSICA JONES
Uh-huh. So you want me to ''out'' Spider-Man and you want Mr. Urich here to report on it for your newspaper.

J. JONAH JAMESON
An onion peel. Do you know what an onion peel is?

JESSICA JONES
I could guess.

J. JONAH JAMESON
We'll follow you as you pull the layers, follow the leads, turn over the rocks. How great will this be? Not only will it be killer journalism -- but money will actually start shooting out of my ass faster than we can print papers.

JESSICA JONES
I'd like to think about it.

J. JONAH JAMESON
Listen, I don't have time to change your tampons for you. I need an answer.

JESSICA JONES
I'm sorry?

J. JONAH JAMESON
In or out, Ms. Jones.

JESSICA JONES
Well, these kinds of investigations are rather unique.

J. JONAH JAMESON
Don't toss my salad -- how much are we talking?

JESSICA JONES
Hard to say. I don't even know where I am going to begin.

J. JONAH JAMESON
Ms. Brant!!

BETTY BRANT
Here -- here -- I was making the copies.

J. JONAH JAMESON
Where's the Spider-Man map?

BETTY BRANT
It's right there.

J. JONAH JAMESON
Right where?

BETTY BRANT
Right under your elbow.

J. JONAH JAMESON
Oh . . .

JESSICA JONES
Map?   Map?

J. JONAH JAMESON
We've taken the liberty of compiling a list and a chart of frequent Spider-Man sightings. Places where he is repeatedly seen. See? Empire State University, Queens . . .

JESSICA JONES
So, I'm not the first investigator you've had on this.

J. JONAH JAMESON
It's a pet project -- as I said -- renewed by this Daredevil news. Here are some pictures that Parker kid took a couple of years back. You can see -- see? You can see some of the same buildings in the background. I think it's Soho.

JESSICA JONES
What happened the last time you tried this.

J. JONAH JAMESON
I'll be blunt with you, Jones. I'm offering you fame and fortune. The kind you weren't able to put together on your own -- even in any of your silly little "identities." One would imagine that off the fumes of a story like this you'll be up to your elbows in "sneaky work" till the cows come home. So, last time, are you in or --?

JESSICA JONES
Sure, I'll do it.

But there is the matter
of an advance.

J. JONAH JAMESON
What is this?

BEN URICH
I don't know -- what is that?

J. JONAH JAMESON
It's Jessica's invoices for the last three weeks.

BEN URICH
Well I told you , Jonah --

J. JONAH JAMESON
What is this?!!

BEN URICH
Jonah -- I'm not in charge of invoicing -- I don't...

J. JONAH JAMESON
What kind of crap are you pulling?

BEN URICH
Me?

J. JONAH JAMESON
Ms. Black from accounting red-flagged this -- this -- this... What the hell is "Mercy's Kitchen"?

BEN URICH
Oh -- uh -- that's that soup kitchen in Hell's Kitchen that she has been --

J. JONAH JAMESON
Soup kitchen in Hell's kitchen?

BEN URICH
Yes. Yeah -- she's been working there for the last three weeks. She's been --

J. JONAH JAMESON
Working there, why?

BEN URICH
Said she had it on a good source that one of the regulars at the kitchen is Spider-Man. She said --

J. JONAH JAMESON
One of the drunken bums who comes into the --

BEN URICH
She said that she planned on gaining the trust of the regulars in hope of finding out who, and --

J. JONAH JAMESON
She serves them lunch?

BEN URICH
Yes.

J. JONAH JAMESON
And what do you do...?

BEN URICH
I --

J. JONAH JAMESON
You sit there and watch?

BEN URICH
And... help.

J. JONAH JAMESON
What?

BEN URICH
Well, there's stuff to do. I --

J. JONAH JAMESON
What? You bus tables?

BEN URICH
Not every day.

J. JONAH JAMESON
Holy God -- Did you
go to college?

BEN URICH
You know I --

J. JONAH JAMESON
Then why the hell are you
busing tables?

BEN URICH
It's a --

J. JONAH JAMESON
Do you know she keeps buying
food for those drunken bums and
billing the paper?

BEN URICH
No, I --

J. JONAH JAMESON
Six hundred dollars for tapioca pudding.

BEN URICH
Oh...

J. JONAH JAMESON
I'm holding a bill for six hundred dollars
for tapioca pudding!!

—or the first time in my decades-
ong career as a -- She's buying
pudding for drunks and trying to
get me to pay for it --

BEN URICH
Well, she did say expenses.

Phone calls and paperclips
are expenses!!! This is pudding!!

BEN URICH
I didn't know she was billing it to you.

Well, she is!! Two hundred dollars an
hour, all day every day!! For her to serve
pudding to meth addicts -- and one of
my best reporters bussing tables!

BEN URICH
Okay. Jessica told me that she asked
around the quote superhero community
and word was that Spider-Man has said
he was an orphan. At these orphanages --
Jessica volunteered. helping out. Reading
some books to the children.

J. JONAH JAMESON
How does reading books to a
bunch of unwanted brats help
her find out about Spider-Man?

BEN URICH
Well , I asked her that. I asked

J. JONAH JAMESON
Uh huh.

ROBBIE ROBERTSON
It's the same for us in
our business.

BEN URICH

BEN URICH
Thanks --

J. JONAH JAMESON
Shut up! Give me the report so far --

BEN URICH
Didn't she send some kind of --

J. JONAH JAMESON
Give me your notes, Urich!!

BEN URICH
Okay, Okay. Here -- uh -- well, soon after you hired her we made the rounds to a handful of orphanages. Three orphanages. St. Alexis' of 49th, The Tony Stark Foundation Home for Wayward --

J. JONAH JAMESON
Come on --

J. JONAH JAMESON
I have a bill here. She bought the kids cupcakes for a week at one of these --

BEN URICH
Then it was on to St. Catherine's Hospital where Jessica said she had a tip that one of the orderlies was Spider-Man. She said it was well known among her circle that he --

J. JONAH JAMESON
So she volunteered at the hospital.

BEN URICH
The AIDS ward.

J. JONAH JAMESON
Pssss...

BEN URICH
And for the last few weeks she's been at the soup kitchen...

J. JONAH JAMESON
Damn it, Urich!

BEN URICH
What?

J. JONAH JAMESON
She's scamming us!!
She's scamming me!!

BEN URICH
How is she --

J. JONAH JAMESON
AIDS patients, orphans, winos!!
Volunteering at two hundred
dollars an hour!

BEN URICH
I --

J. JONAH JAMESON
Were you ever there when she got
one of these little "tips" of hers?

BEN URICH
The actual tip? No. It was after --

J. JONAH JAMESON
Did you ever see any of her
so called super hero pals?

BEN URICH
Uh -- no.

J. JONAH JAMESON
No?

BEN URICH
No.

J. JONAH JAMESON
You stupid, WORTHLESS,
WASTE OF --

ROBBIE ROBERTSON
Jonah!

J. JONAH JAMESON
Dammit! She scammed us!
A damn scam artist!

ROBBIE ROBERTSON
Jonah --

BEN URICH
Well maybe if --

J. JONAH JAMESON
What??!!

BEN URICH
Nothing.

ROBBIE ROBERTSON
What Ben was going to say is --
that maybe when you hired her if
you hadn't insulted every single
facet of her life --

J. JONAH JAMESON
What?

ROBBIE ROBERTSON
Jonah. You . . .

J. JONAH JAMESON
What did I say?

ROBBIE ROBERTSON
You said that superheroes
deserve to be --

J. JONAH JAMESON
I say that in the paper
every freaking day.

ROBBIE ROBERTSON
You said that private investigators
are pieces of --

J. JONAH JAMESON
They are! She knows that.
Doesn't mean she can steal
from me --

ROBBIE ROBERTSON
Jonah --

J. JONAH JAMESON
Stole money out of me --

ROBBIE ROBERTSON
Jonah, you can't prove that.

J. JONAH JAMESON
What?

ROBBIE ROBERTSON
They are legitimate --

J. JONAH JAMESON
Shut up!

ROBBIE ROBERTSON
Legitimate claims --

J. JONAH JAMESON
Well, I'm not buying
this pudding.

ROBBIE ROBERTSON
You signed a contract with
the woman.

J. JONAH JAMESON
Ms. Brant!! Get in here!!

ROBBIE ROBERTSON
You signed a contract --

J. JONAH JAMESON
You know what, Ben? You write
your damn story -- you tell
the world what this lying --

ROBBIE ROBERTSON
That she what? Fed the homeless,
read to orphans, and cared for
AIDS patients?

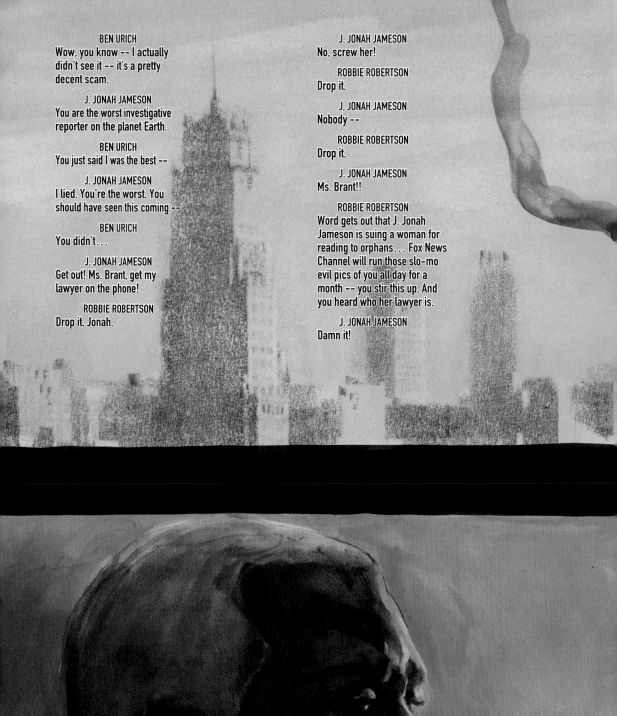

BEN URICH
Wow, you know -- I actually didn't see it -- it's a pretty decent scam.

J. JONAH JAMESON
You are the worst investigative reporter on the planet Earth.

BEN URICH
You just said I was the best --

J. JONAH JAMESON
I lied. You're the worst. You should have seen this coming --

BEN URICH
You didn't...

J. JONAH JAMESON
Get out! Ms. Brant, get my lawyer on the phone!

ROBBIE ROBERTSON
Drop it, Jonah.

J. JONAH JAMESON
No, screw her!

ROBBIE ROBERTSON
Drop it.

J. JONAH JAMESON
Nobody --

ROBBIE ROBERTSON
Drop it.

J. JONAH JAMESON
Ms. Brant!!

ROBBIE ROBERTSON
Word gets out that J. Jonah Jameson is suing a woman for reading to orphans... Fox News Channel will run those slo-mo evil pics of you all day for a month -- you stir this up. And you heard who her lawyer is.

J. JONAH JAMESON
Damn it!

ROBBIE ROBERTSON
Drop it.

J, JONAH JAMESON
Damn it!

ROBBIE ROBERTSON
Just chalk it up --

J. JONAH JAMESON
Damn super heroes --
every time.

ROBBIE ROBERTSON
All right, I'm going home.

J. JONAH JAMESON
Ms. Brant, get me that woman's
telephone number -- oh here
it is -- I got it! Never mind!

ROBBIE ROBERTSON
Jonah...

J. JONAH JAMESON
Oh no! Oh no! the least I get
to do -- the least I get to do
is let her know I know and
that the jig is up!

ROBBIE ROBERTSON
I don't think --

J. JONAH JAMESON
It's her machine. Doesn't
even have the guts to --
Ms. Jones, this is J. Jonah
Jameson, publisher of
the Daily Bugle.

J. JONAH JAMESON
I just want you to know that your
services are no longer required.

I know who you are and I know
what you tried to pull. You think
you're all clever? Well, let me
tell you something, Missy.
You aren't clever.

ROBBIE ROBERTSON
Hang up the phone, Jonah.

J. JONAH JAMESON
And I pray -- I get down on my
hands and knees and I pray for the
day that you screw up somewhere
because my paper will be so far
up your nose that -- that -- that --
arrgghhh! I hate you!

ROBBIE ROBERTSON
Hang up, Jonah.

J. JONAH JAMESON
And you probably knew who
Spider-Man was the entire time --
you and your little secret
superfriends. Well, I hope you
take your money and I hope
you superchoke on it.
Coff!! Aagh! Damn cigar!

ALIAS
INVESTIGATIONS

daughter ndoval &
The warm
Bavaria

featuring
"On The L

IF YOU HaD
A WiSH

WHAT WOULD iT Be?

the best future is

the one we walk into well-

MAKE IT HAPPEN

We're sitting there in his limo.

And I'm waiting... waiting for a response from him.

And nothing.

He just sits there Which is the exact opposite of what he was like the last time I met him when he wouldn't shut his fucking mouth.

And then I start reminding myself how much I don't want to be sitting here with this piece of garbage.

All I hear in my head is: This guy hates you.

And this isn't like my usual self-loathing paranoia. No.

I have it on tape. On my answering machine. Him wishing I would drop dead.

This guy-- this rich, asshole scumbag.

He's everything that's wrong with journalism in America. Guy with a clear agenda and he uses his Daily Bugle as a forum to express it instead of reporting the facts.

Disgusting.

I'm sitting there thinking... this piece of garbage.

And believe me, if this was about him... Fuck 'im!

But it's not. It's about a girl.

It's about some girl I know nothing about named Matti Franklin. A girl that he somehow took responsibility for who is now in some kind of trouble.

And I sat there in silence.

And I didn't know what else to do.

Regardless, I was in the situation I was in now and the best thing I could think to do is try to find the girl.

How?

Well, I'm a private investigator... basically I just start throwing shit at the wall and I see if anything sticks.

I went back to my office and I started making a point list of everything I heard or saw since this shit began. I wrote down everything I remember this Mattie saying.

They-- they lied to me! Those fuckers lied to me! Sniff!

I looked over the very brief file I had on her.

Then I wrote down everything I remember Jameson saying.

ALIAS INVESTIGATIONS

Name: Mattie Franklin
ID: Secret (Minor)
Last known residence: Jameson,
Powers: 'Psychic' Spider Legs (Se
Flight (6). Strength and Agility (1
Comments: Participant in the
"Gathering Of Five" incident. (See
Ritual involving five people biddi
for power through the combining
five ancient artifacts.
Associates: MadameWeb
Jessica Drew (

Well, Jameson always has a gay boner for Spider-Man.

And I bet he mentioned Daredevil just because he's in the news.

But Osborn. Norman Osborn? Is he even still alive?

Spider-Man. Spider-Woman.

Spider-Woman.

Jessica Drew?

Jessica's name is in Mattie's tiny S.H.I.E.L.D. file.

What is this other name? Madame Web.

Madame Web? What the fuck is a Madame Web?

Jessica Drew. Jessica Drew.

Spider-Man! Daredevil! Osborn!! All of you!!!

CONFIDENTIAL

Didn't set my alarm. Fell asleep on my couch like an asshole.

Thank God I got up in time to shower and get over to my actually paying job this month.

I don't usually bodyguard-- even though a lot of P.I.s do. I don't like to do it. It's grunt work. Mindless bullshit.

But for my attorney, Matt Murdock, I'll do it. He's certainly been there for me enough times-- and he's going through a real bunch of crap now.

The tabloids outted him as Daredevil. Can you believe that shit? They just outted him. "The man without fear" outted as a blind Hell's Kitchen lawyer.

("Man without fear"-- I had nothing that cool in my flying days.)

They outted him, but he is publicly standing up to it. He's denying the whole thing and suing the shit out of everybody.

Good for him. Fuck the assholes.

So he needs me, and a couple of others like Luke Cage, to hang around the office, walk him to work.

We're supposed to keep an eye out for any of Daredevil's asshole butt-buddy rogue's gallery who might come around looking for some mindless payback-- but none of them have shown up.

All we end up doing all day is pushing the media away from him.

But he asks me to be here-- I'm here. Hate taking his money but he won't let me *not* take it.

And I need it.

He has it and I need it.

The only thing that really irritates me about this gig is that any asshole with two eyes can see that he really *is* Daredevil-- and that I am just here for show.

But he hasn't confided in me.

He knows I know, but he just won't come out and tell me.

Think he told Luke Cage. But he won't tell me.

Sexist shit.

But this is the little revenge game I play with him.

Everyday I refuse to knock on the door.

I just stand down here.

I know that his Daredevil powers will "see" me here. Whatever they are, they must be able to if he can do all those things as Daredevil.

And out he will come.

We do this everyday.

I also light up just to be a bitch. He should fucking trust me more.

Good morning, Jessica.

Mornin'.

Haven't seen you in a couple of days. How's everything?

Living a dream.

Aaand... I think I got in trouble again.

Legal trouble?

Maybe. Do you know who J. Jonah Jameson is?

Not one of my favorite people.

I don't think he's one of *his* favorite people.

What happened?

Short version: a girl, a runaway by the looks of it, who was staying with the Jamesons-- turns out she's really this teenage Spider-Woman.

Yeah.

With super powers and a costume?

Looks like.

Jameson had a super hero girl living in his house?

That she had powers?

Wow, that's-- did he know?

Have no idea. Don't think so.

Yeah.

You met her?

I don't know--

Sadly, yeah.

So, I don't understand... he lives at home with you, or--?

He did up 'til six months ago. Not no more.

He got a fancy condo and all that. And he's dating his teeny super hero girl and peddling whatever he is peddling.

In passing, at the mall. She seemed out of it, so I imagine he is keeping her 'well medicated'.

I mean, how else's she going to stand barking on all fours for him?

I mean-- Eew.

Dazzler.

I guess.

His buddy Ivan nailed her last year, so I know that Denny has been itching for his own super hero girlfriend.

But, see, Malcolm told my friend that you're looking for her and I imagine her parents are, too.

And if she's shacked up with my asshole brother, all strung out, and you can get her home-- then go to, man.

Do you have your brother's address?

Thing is, he has this image in his head of what *success* should look like.

And he's been partnered up with this Lithuanian dude Ivan-- and Ivan fucked that one disco skank.

The one with the-- the one who could make the lights.

Even a little one.

Sick, ain't it? Any guy ever do that to you?

No, he ain't ever let me over.

I told you-- he's been a way huge prick lately.

But--

--he hangs out at this club or something... Club 616 or something.

Him and his partner. They always there.

So, I get the job?

Let me look into it.

ISSUE #19

It's her.

Mattie Franklin.

Spider-Woman.

It's her and she looks right at me.

Crap! I didn't expect her to be here. She's only a kid. This is a nightclub and she's only a kid.

I was looking for her boyfriend here-- get to him to get to her-- but here she is.

A costume? In a nightclub? What the fuck is going on here? What is she on?

She's looking right at me.

The jig is up. I'm going to have to grab her and run.

Fuck, though.

I don't know what the story is here-- I don't know who is who. If I just grab her and run, someone might get hurt.

Or these a-holes might come looking for her at the Jamesons', where she lives-- and I-- ugghh!!

I don't know what to do.

Jesus, she looks even worse than she did in my apartment a couple of days ago.

What is she on? Heroin?

I want to cry just from looking at her. She looks right at me, but-- is she so out of it she doesn't recognize me?

Maybe it's the outfit and incredibly whorish makeup I put on to get into this trendy fuckhole.

Mattie Franklin. It's hard to believe she's a super hero.

Kids shouldn't be super heroes-- look at her. God damn, on my worst day I never looked that bad.

That fucker.

You've been following me? God.

He thinks you have his girl, Mattie...

I know.

...but I know you don't.

I just want to figure out exactly what--

Ow...

What happened?

I fucking *had* her. I *had* her.

Who?

Mattie Franklin. I found her.

She was *here*?

She was right in there.

I-- I was-- was-- was frozen in *shock* over what I saw and I--

She was with these guys and when I went to grab her they punched my fucking-- ow!

I thought you have powers.

I do.

They did too.

I guess. Ow.

I've never been punched that hard-- and I've been punched.

What was Mattie doing?

Oh, man, she's totally strung out.

She's-- they got her on something.

These guys-- they got her on something and they're popping pills and they-- oh, God.

Have they harmed her?

Yes.

>Sniff< God...

Did they have protruded foreheads? The guys?

Yes.

MGH. They're fucking animals.

MGH? I don't know what that is.

(Ow.)

Mutant Growth Hormone. It's expensive shit. It's a street drug.

But supposedly, it temporarily-- for the length of the high-- it gives normal people not so normal abilities.

Oh, fuck me. Are you *serious*?

There's all kinds of different mixtures and ways to freebase it.

The pure stuff-- pure from the course-- is like gold.

Crazy fuckers.

The foreheads are the giveaway.

They're fucking up their genetic makeup with that shit. Their cell structure is damaged.

They cut her.

I know. It's sickening. It's cannibalistic.

This is going on?

There's been rumblings about a couple of B-level super heroes-- no offense-- selling parts of themselves, or trading it for who-knows-what.

I heard Darkhawk might be.

They are killing that girl. I lost her.

We have to-- we have to--

I thought you weren't a super hero anymore.

'M not.

Anybody paying you to find her?

Short of being chopped in half and waking up to find out that I have been turned into a half woman/ half robot cyborg...

..I can't imagine how that little adventure could have gone any worse.

The cops were so goddamn condescending. Bunch o' fucking power-tripping motherfuckers.

I enjoyed every bullshit lie I told them about how I was mugged.

Fuckers.

Fuck them!

Treat a woman like she's a child that shouldn't be out after dark.

Jake's

Eff you, little-dick, badge-wearing assholes.

Do your job!!

That whole thing was fucking awful.

I hope that Urich guy finds out something about where Mattie is, and I hope he tells Jonah to leave me alone.

I just want to get that girl home safe. Then I want to be left alone.

My body can't take this kind of abuse. I'm not that kind of person. I don't have the--

Jonah... Please forgive my husband...

They warned us. Everybody warned us that taking in an orphan was going to be trouble.

She could run away, lash out at us... the anger, the hostility...

...not understanding who you are or why life has dealt you a shit hand.

I'm an orphan.

You're Ms. Jones, the woman who last saw Mattie.

Yes, ma'am.

I was the one who originally approached your husband about Mattie's disappearance.

But because of some misunderstandings we've had in the past, he mistook my words as-- as some sort of threat.

And you are?

Jessica Drew. I am friends with Mattie... in her other life.

I was looking for her as well.

You're the original Spider-Woman.

Yes, ma'am.

And what Mr. Urich told us about what they are doing to her...

This is true, Ms. Jones? You saw this with your own eyes?

Yes, ma'am.

I am sorry to say, yes.

I thought that if anyone should tell Jonah about what Mattie could do, it should be Mattie.

You know now that she dressed as Spider-Man?

That is going to be a hard pill for Jonah to swallow. Hopefully, we will deal with that when we get her back home safe.

How long exactly has she been missing?

A couple of weeks, we think.

You *think*?

This building is a secure fortress. We just-- oh, God...

If we call the police, Jonah's enemies-- they will tear this girl apart.

They will *mock* and ridicule her.

Call her a junkie and a whore. All to get at Jonah.

They are waiting-- they have been waiting for a moment *just* like this.

We are both professional people. Working. We aren't always home at dinnertime and Mattie had proven herself *very* independent and very *resourceful*.

We're bad parents.

We didn't know. We *didn't* know!!!

But we *will* call the police. We will do whatever we can to save her.

But if first you-- if you could help...

If you could get Mattie back for us before they kill her.

Before they--

If you could do this...

Please... could you do this?

Shit!

...heeey, man, what's goin' on?

Mattie? Sweetie? It's me, Jessica Drew.

Noooo shit. Hey, girl.

Hey...

BAM BAM BAM

Open up!!

BAM BAM BAM

I gotta get her out of here before the cops--

Let them in.

Shut up!

Hey, I was a New Warrior, man!

Police! Open the door!!

BAM

What should I do?

Freeze! Police!!

Shit!

Drop the girl, scumbag!!

Next: the secret origins of jessica jones

CONFIDENTIAL